*Why Is This Night
Different from
All Other Nights?*

Why Is This Night Different from All Other Nights?

"THE FOUR QUESTIONS" AROUND THE WORLD

Ilana Kurshan

Introduction by Rabbi Joseph Telushkin

SCHOCKEN BOOKS   NEW YORK

Library of Congress Cataloging-in-Publication Data

Mah nishtannah. Polyglot.
Why is this night different from all other nights ? :
"the Four questions" around the world / Ilana Kurshan.

p. cm.

The Four questions translated into 23 different languages,
with accompanying text in English.

ISBN 978-0-8052-4252-2

1. Seder—Liturgy—Texts.   2. Judaism—Liturgy—Texts.
3. Jews—History.   I. Kurshan, Llana.   II. Title.

BM670.M32K8712 2008

296.4'5371—dc22   2007036643

www.schocken.com
Book design by Virginia Tan
Printed in the United States of America
First Edition
2 4 6 8 9 7 5 3 1

מַה־נִּשְׁתַּנָּה הַלַּיְלָה הַזֶּה מִכָּל־הַלֵּילוֹת?

שֶׁבְּכָל־הַלֵּילוֹת אָנוּ אוֹכְלִין חָמֵץ וּמַצָּה; הַלַּיְלָה הַזֶּה כֻּלּוֹ מַצָּה.

שֶׁבְּכָל־הַלֵּילוֹת אָנוּ אוֹכְלִין שְׁאָר יְרָקוֹת; הַלַּיְלָה הַזֶּה מָרוֹר.

שֶׁבְּכָל־הַלֵּילוֹת אֵין אָנוּ מַטְבִּילִין אֲפִילוּ פַּעַם אֶחָת; הַלַּיְלָה הַזֶּה שְׁתֵּי פְעָמִים.

שֶׁבְּכָל־הַלֵּילוֹת אָנוּ אוֹכְלִין בֵּין יוֹשְׁבִין וּבֵין מְסֻבִּין; הַלַּיְלָה הַזֶּה כֻּלָּנוּ מְסֻבִּין.

Why is this night different from all other nights?

On all other nights we eat both leavened and unleavened bread;
on this night we eat only unleavened bread.

On all other nights we eat all kinds of vegetables;
on this night we eat only bitter herbs.

On all other nights we do not dip our food even once;
on this night we dip our food twice.

On all other nights we eat either seated straight or reclining;
on this night we eat only reclining.

Contents

Ma Nishtana

INTRODUCTION BY RABBI JOSEPH TELUSHKIN

A N OLD JEWISH JOKE. A distinguished Jewish writer in England is contacted by Buckingham Palace and informed that at an upcoming ceremony he will be knighted by the queen. A protocol official from the palace meets with him and explains that when he is standing before the queen, just before he is knighted, there is a formulaic phrase in Latin he must recite.

The great day arrives, and the writer waits his turn as one person after another steps up in front of the queen, recites the phrase, and is knighted. Finally, he finds himself in front of the queen, but the Latin words totally flee his mind. Precious seconds are ticking by, and, finally, the only non-English words he knows come tripping off his tongue: *"Ma nishtana ha'laila ha'zeh meekol ha'leilot."*

The puzzled queen turns to her protocol official and asks: "Why is this knight different from all other knights?"

. . .

I HAVE NEVER told this joke to a Jewish audience and not received a big laugh, which is unusual if only because there is no other extended Hebrew phrase (with the exception of the first line of the *Sh'ma*) that I would tell a Jewish audience without feeling the need to translate. Thus, although many Jews recognize the word *Bereshit* as the first word of the Bible, many don't, and I would never use the word in a speech without explaining that it means "in the beginning." The *Ma Nishtana*, however, is an exception. Because it is traditionally recited by children, Jews remember it their entire lives. Indeed, for many Jewish children, the *Ma Nishtana* represents their first public performance. I don't know this to be true for a fact, but I would guess that the recitation of the *Ma Nishtana* might have been the first time that singers such as Barbra Streisand, Bette Middler, and Neil Sedaka revealed their voices in a public setting.

What is also interesting, and characteristically Jewish, is that this first public performance is composed of questions. Questions have played a critical role in Jewish life from the very beginning. In the Bible they are often directed to God. Abraham, the first Jew, challenges God: "Shall not the judge of all the earth act justly?" (Genesis 18:25). And the prophet Jeremiah similarly challenges God with a question that, in one form or another, is still regularly posed to God and believers alike: "Why does the way of the wicked prosper?" (Jeremiah 12:1).

However, unlike these demanding theological questions, the Four Questions of the *Ma Nishtana* are directed not at God but at one's parents. And like the question posed by the Wise Son in the Haggadah, the queries in the *Ma Nishtana* presuppose that the questioner intends to observe the holiday's rituals but simply wants a greater understanding of how and why to do so.

In my almost sixty years I have attended well over a hundred sedarim, and my experience is that very few fathers or mothers take the time to explain to the boy or girl reciting the *Ma Nishtana* the answers to these Four Questions. Which leads to a second Jewish joke:

The night of the seder arrives, and the family expectantly waits for young Judah to recite the *Ma Nishtana,* as he has done for the preceding two years. But the boy doesn't move. His parents motion for Judah to stand, but he remains in his seat. Finally, they tell him to rise and recite the *Ma Nishtana.* "I won't do it," the boy says.

The parents and all the guests are shocked. "Why not?"

"Every year I ask the Four Questions," the boy explains, "and Papa never answers them. It's clear he doesn't know the answers. So I'm not going to ask again. It's not nice for Papa."

THE TRUTH IS there are plenty of papas, and mamas, who don't know the answers to the Four Questions, particularly the third. So as my Passover gift this year to Jewish parents, here are the Four Questions and at least one person's version of the correct responses:

Question: Why is it that on all other nights we eat both leavened bread and matzah, but on this night we eat only matzah?

Answer: When the Jews were fleeing Egypt, they didn't have time to wait for the bread to rise, so they removed the bread from the ovens while it was still flat and took it with them. Among other things, the eating of matzah symbolizes that it is better to eat a "poor man's bread" and be free, than to eat a tasty loaf of bread and live in slavery.

Question: Why is it that on all other nights we eat all kinds of vegetables, but on this night we eat only bitter herbs?

Answer: We eat the maror, the bitter herb, to remind us of the bitterness of the slavery our ancestors endured in Egypt.

Question: Why is it that on all other nights we do not dip our vegetables even once, but on this night we dip them twice?

Answer: The two dippings refer to the dipping early in the seder of the green vegetable into salt water and the dipping later in the seder of the bitter herb into the charoset, the sweet mixture of nuts, wine, and fruit. The salt water in which the first vegetable is dipped symbolizes the tears shed by the oppressed slaves, while the sweet charoset represents an attempt to lessen the bitterness of the maror.

Question: Why is it that on all other nights we either sit or recline at the dinner table, but on this night we eat only in a reclining position?

Answer: The reason we are instructed to recline is that in the world of the Romans, who were the dominant world power when the Haggadah was formally composed, this was how free men sat at the table, and so eating in a reclining position came to symbolize for the rabbis a sense of luxury and freedom. This is no longer the custom in our world today, but observant Jews do still drink the four cups of wine and eat most of the ritual foods (if not the entire meal) while in a semireclining position (it helps to have a pillow between your back and the chair).

JEWISH CHILDREN have been reciting the *Ma Nishtana* for about a hundred generations and, as this book makes clear, in many different countries. But of one thing we can be sure: As long as children are chanting these questions, the Jewish people will go on.

May all of us merit to celebrate our sedarim in an atmosphere of freedom, and may we all merit to hear our nephews and nieces, our children, our children's children, and even our grandchildren's children chant the *Ma Nishtana*. For truly this night is different from all other nights, and the *Ma Nishtana* is one of the key elements that makes it so.

Why Is This Night
Different from
All Other Nights?

Afrikaans

Black South African teachers observe a class at the King David School,
a Jewish day school in Johannesburg, through an arrangement made by
South Africa's Union of Jewish Women, 1979.

*(Johannesburg, South African Jewish Board of Deputies.
Photo courtesy of Beth Hatefutsoth Photo Archive, Tel Aviv)*

Waarom is hierdie nag
anders as al die ander nagte?

Op al die nagte (van die jaar) mag ons gesuurde
of ongesuurde brood eet; maar hierdie nag net
ongesuurde brood.

Op al die nagte mag ons enige soort kruie eet;
maar hierdie nag net bitter kruie.

Op al die nagte doop ons selfs nie eenmaal iets in
nie; maar hierdie nag doop ons twee maal in.

Op al die nagte eet ons óf sittend óf leunend;
maar die nag leun ons almal.

THE JEWS OF SOUTH AFRICA

AFRIKAANS is one of the official languages of South Africa, where Jews have been living for nearly three hundred years. The first Jewish immigrants, from England and Germany, worked for the Dutch East India Company, which set up a colony in South Africa in 1652. But it took another 150 years for the Dutch rulers to grant freedom of religion to all peoples, and only then did Jews begin arriving in significant numbers.

The early Jewish immigrants settled mostly in Cape Town and in the eastern parts of the country, where they were active in economic and civic life as merchants, traders, shopkeepers, and peddlers. The first congregation was founded in Cape Town in 1841. It was called Tikvath Israel ("Hope of Israel"), a reference to the Cape of Good Hope at the tip of the continent.

When diamonds and gold were discovered in South Africa in 1867, Jews began to arrive from Western Europe, Australia, and America. More than 40,000 Jews immigrated to South Africa between 1880 and 1910, including refugees from tsarist persecution in Eastern Europe.

In 1910, four colonies were united under the British flag to form the Union of South Africa. Jews encountered immigration restrictions and mild discrimination in the face of their growing numbers. In the 1930s, when several thousand refugees arrived from Nazi Germany, anti-Jewish sentiment reached its peak. The general attitude toward the Jews improved only after World War II, when the official opposition party, the National Party, pledged to stop supporting anti-Semitic policies.

Many of South Africa's Jews, among them Nadine Gordimer and Helen Suzman, were active in the movement to end the South African government's policy of racial discrimination known as apartheid. One of the great leaders of the antiapartheid movement, former president Nelson Mandela, commented. "I have found Jews to be more broad-minded than most whites on issues of race and politics, perhaps because they themselves have historically been victims of prejudice."

In recent times, large numbers of South African Jews have immigrated to Israel. One of the most famous South African Jews to make aliyah was the statesman and diplomat Abba Eban, who was born in Cape Town in 1915. There are about 70,000 Jews living in South Africa today.

Amharic

Right to left: Religious leaders Qes Saghi Baiene, Qes Abbe Brahan,
and Abd Shlomo Abete celebrate the seder in the synagogue in Wolleka,
Ethiopia (a village near Gondar), 1984.

(Doron Bacher, Beth Hatefutsoth. Beth Hatefutsoth Photo Archive, Tel Aviv)

Yichen lelit keleloch/lelitoch hulu lemin teleye?

Beleloch lelitoch huku and gize enkuan aninekrim/maror;
bezich lelit gin hulet gize/eninekralen.

Beleloch hulu yalboka woyim yeboka kita enbelalen;
bezich lelit gin hulu yalboka kita bicha.

Beleloch hulu leloch kitelakitelochin hulu enbelalen;
bezich gize gin merara bicha.

Beleloch hulu tekemten woyim zimbel bilen enbelalen enitetalen;
bezich lelit gin hulachin zenbel bilen neew.

ይህን ለሊት /ከሌሎች/ ለሉቶች ሁሉ በምን ተለየ?

በሌሎች ለሊቶች ሁሉ አንድ ጊዜስ እንኳን አንነከርም/ማሮር/በዚህ ለሊት ግን ሁለት ጊዜ /እንነከራለን/።

በሌሎች ሁሉ ያልቦባ ወይም የቦካ ቂጣ እንበላለን። በዚህ ለሊት ግን ሁሉ ያልቦካ ቂጣ ብቻ።

በሌሎች ሁሉ ሌሎች ቅጠላ ቅጠሎችን ሁሉ እንበላለን፤ በዚህ ጊዜ ግን መራራ ብቻ።

በሌሎች ሁሉ ተቀምጠን ወይም ዘንበል ብለን እንበላለን፤ እንጠጣለንም። በዚህ ለሊት ግን ሁላችን ዘንበል ብለን ነው።

THE JEWS OF ETHIOPIA

Amharic is the language spoken by about a third of the population of Ethiopia, where the Jewish community is known as Beta Israel. According to the biblical book of Kings, the Ethiopian queen of Sheba visited King Solomon in the tenth century B.C.E. to witness his great wisdom. This legend is recounted in the *Kebra Nagast*, a classic fourteenth-century account of ancient Ethiopian history, which relates that their relationship resulted in the birth of a son, Menelik, who brought Jewish customs to Ethiopia. According to another tradition, the Beta Israel are descended from the tribe of Dan, one of the ten "lost" tribes exiled by the Assyrians from the Kingdom of Israel in 722 B.C.E. Still another theory maintains that they are descendants of Ethiopian Christians and pagans who converted to Judaism centuries ago.

In the fifth century C.E., Christianity spread throughout Ethiopia, but the Beta Israel continued to practice Judaism and to enjoy general independence. In the thirteenth century, the reigning Christian kings claimed to be descended from King Solomon, adopted the Lion of Judah as their emblem, and began a series of intermittent wars against the Beta Israel. In 1622, the Christians conquered the Ethiopian Jewish kingdom. Most of the Jews were sold as slaves, forced to accept baptism, and denied the right to own land. But a remnant of the community remained intact. In 1867, Professor Joseph Halévy became the first European Jew to visit the Beta Israel. And in 1908, rabbis from forty-four countries confirmed that the Beta Israel were authentic Jews.

A 1974 coup against Emperor Haile Selassie, who considered himself a descendant of King Solomon, led to widespread violence and political instability. Three years later, approximately 8,000 Ethiopian Jews were airlifted to Israel. In 1984, they were joined by another 6,500 Jews in a massive, secret airlift known as Operation Moses. But the most significant Ethiopian aliyah took place in May 1991 with Operation Solomon, in which 14,000 Ethiopian Jews were secretly transported to Israel in thirty-four El Al airplanes in just over thirty-six hours. Today, more than 90,000 members of the Beta Israel live in Israel. Very few remain in Ethiopia, and efforts are under way to bring them to Israel, too.

Chinese

Chinese policemen in the Hongkew District of Shanghai inspect a consignment of matzot in the bicycle basket of a Jewish refugee, 1947.

(H. Eisfelder, Carnegie, Australia. Beth Hatefutsoth Photo Archive,
Tel Aviv. Courtesy of H. Eisfelder, Carnegie, Australia)

Wei shen mo jin wen bu tong yu qi ta yie wen?

Mei wen women chi mian bao he bing;
dan jin wen women zhi chi bing.

Mei wen women you hen duo bu tong zhong de qing cai;
dan jin wen women zhi chi ku cai.

Mei wen women bu bi jin pao mian bao huo bing;
dan jin wen women yao jin pao liang ci.

Mei ci wen fan women ke yi zuo zhi huo sui yi xie kao;
dan jin wen women yi zhi ke yi sui yi xie kao zhe chi.

为什么这夜与其他夜不同？

在其他夜我们吃发酵的和未膨松面制面包；这夜我们仅吃未膨松面制面包。

在其他夜我们吃各种各样的蔬菜；这夜我们仅吃苦涩草根。

在其他夜晚餐时我们根本不浸泡我们的食物；这夜我们要浸泡二次。

在其他夜我们吃晚餐时坐直或斜靠；这夜的整个晚餐中，我们舒服地斜靠。

THE JEWS OF CHINA

ACCORDING TO archaeological evidence, the first Jews in China came from Persia in the eighth century. In 1163, the emperor ordered the Jews to live in Kaifeng, a city along the Yellow River in northeast China. Chinese Jews were allowed to choose from among only seven last names, and, to this day, all Chinese Jews have one of these names.

Jews continued to live in Kaifeng for several centuries. Travelers such as Marco Polo, who visited China in the thirteenth century, reported on the Jewish presence in China and commented that Mongol conqueror Kublai Khan observed the festivals of the Jews, Christians, and Muslims.

Westerners lost contact with the Chinese Jewish community until the eighteenth century, when Jesuit missionaries arrived and recorded their meetings with Chinese Jews. During the Taiping rebellion of the 1850s, the Jews of Kaifeng suffered and were dispersed. Following this dislocation, they returned to Kaifeng, yet they remained small in number and continued to face hardships.

A significant subset of the Chinese Jewish community consisted of Russian Jews, who came fleeing pogroms in the nineteenth century. They founded Jewish communities in Harbin, Tianjin, and elsewhere. Other Jews came because they were granted incentives to settle in

China by the Russian government, which sought to populate the city of Harbin, where the project to construct a Russian railway to East Asia was centered.

Another important Jewish community developed in Shanghai, a port city in eastern China that opened to foreign trade in 1842. Many of the first Jewish immigrants to this city were Sephardic Jews from Iraq; others came from India, especially Bombay. They played a significant role in developing the opium and cotton trades, among other industries. Another wave of Jews came to Shanghai in the 1930s, mostly from Germany, Austria, and Poland.

The Japanese captured Shanghai in 1937 and closed it to further immigration in December 1941. They deported most of the Jews to the Hongkew District and kept them in unsanitary semi-internment camps under Japanese occupation forces. The Shanghai Jews suffered great economic and property loss during the war, after which most left for the United States, Britain, Israel, Australia, and other countries.

Today, the Jewish community in China has a population of about one thousand, nearly all of whom live in Shanghai.

Czech

This statue of the Golem of Prague appears at the entrance
to the Town Hall in Prague, which was built in 1912.

*(Daniel Ophir, Israel. Beth Hatefutsoth Photo Archive, Tel Aviv.
Courtesy of Dani Ophir, Israel)*

Próach yest veéznamenanah táto noats zeh fshekh nótsee?*

F'kázhdeh yéneh nótsee smeémeh yeéstee kísaneh ee nékisaneh; f'téhto nótsee yen nékisaneh.

F'kázhdeh yéneh nótsee smeémeh yeéstee fshékhnee droóhe bílin; f'téhto nótsee yen hórshkeh bílinee.

F'kázhdeh yéneh nótsee áhnee yédno nénamacheemeh (péhterzheleh doe sláneh vódee ah zhézhikhee doe slótkeh smnyésee); f'téhto nótsee dvákrateh.

F'kázhdeh yéneh nótsee smeémeh yeéstee spsheémuh sédeetseh néboh sótseh ópshenee; f'téhto nótsee yen sótseh ópshenee.

*transliteration

Proč jest vyznamenána talo noc ze všech nocí?

V každé jiné noci smíme jísti kysané i nekysané;
v této noci jen nekysané.

V každé jiné noci smíme jísti všechny druhy bylin;
v této noci jen hořké byliny.

V každé jiné noci ani jednou nenamáčíme (petržele do slané vody a
řeřichy do sladké směsi); této noci dvakráte.

V každé jiné noci smíme jísti zpřima sedíce nebo jsouce opřeni;
této noci jen jsouce opřeni.

THE REGION now known as the Czech Republic has been home to Jews since at least the tenth century. In the eleventh and twelfth centuries, many of the Jews living in what were then known as Bohemia and Moravia were massacred or forced to convert by the Crusader armies marching across Europe. Those Jews who survived were granted only limited civil rights and were forced to live in designated areas, resulting in the creation of a Jewish ghetto.

The situation improved in the early fourteenth century, when Emperor Charles IV protected the Jews from oppression by the local nobility. But in 1389, nearly the entire Jewish population of Prague was massacred at the encouragement of the Christian clergy. By the fifteenth century, Jews were forced to pledge allegiance to various groups of landowners and merchants, and to give them money in return for support and protection.

The late fifteenth century marked the start of a golden age for the Jews. The first Hebrew printing press, famous for its Passover Haggadah, was established in Prague in 1514. One of the most famous Jewish scholars and mystics of the period was Rabbi Judah Loew ben Bezalel, known as the Maharal (1513–1609). According to legend, Rabbi Loew created a Golem—an artificial clay man whom he brought to life through kabbalistic incantations—to protect the Jews of Prague from an upcoming pogrom.

In 1782, Emperor Joseph II issued an Edict of Toleration, which allowed Jews to participate in Bohemian economic and academic life. In 1852, the ghetto was abolished, and Jews gradually became emancipated. By 1900, the Jewish population of Bohemia was divided between speakers of Czech and speakers of German, and Jews became part of the conflict between these two national groups. One of the most famous German-speaking Jews of Prague was the writer Franz Kafka.

In March 1939, Germany attacked and occupied what was then known as Czechoslavakia. About 26,000 Jews escaped, but 92,000 remained. Most were sent to concentration camps, in particular to Theresienstadt, an internment camp about forty miles north of Prague, which served as a way station to Auschwitz. By the end of World War II, only 13,000 Czech Jews remained, and by 1950, about half of them left the then communist-ruled country and immigrated to Israel.

There are about 3,000 Jews in the Czech Republic today. Since the fall of communism in 1990, Jewish life has experienced a bit of a revival, as Jews have become less hesitant about revealing their Jewish ancestry.

Danish

Several generations of the Besbroda family of Copenhagen,
Denmark, at their seder, 1917.

(Beth Hatefutsoth Photo Archive, Tel Aviv. Courtesy of Mrs. A. Besbroda, Denmark)

Hvor er dog denne aften anderledes end
alle andre aftener?

Alle andre aftener spiser vi syret og usyret;
denne aften er alt usyret.

Alle andre aftener spiser vi alle slags urter;
denne aften særlig bitre urter.

Alle andre aftener dypper vi end ikke en eneste gang;
denne aften to gange.

Alle andre aftener spiser vi såvel frit siddende som tilbagelænede;
denne aften er vi alle tilbagelænede.

THE JEWS OF DENMARK

DENMARK was the first Scandinavian country in which Jews were permitted to settle. In 1622, King Christian IV invited the Sephardic Jews of Amsterdam and Hamburg to settle in the recently established Danish township of Glückstadt. Some Jews accepted his invitation and began working in manufacturing and commerce, eventually becoming financiers and jewelers to the royal family.

In the seventeenth and eighteenth centuries, Jews were valued by the government for their beneficial effect on the economy. But several discriminatory measures were put into effect because trade guilds feared Jewish competition. The beginning of the eighteenth century witnessed a spate of mob violence against individual Jews and an attempt to set up ghettos and institute a special tax on the Jews. In 1747, as a result of Christian mistrust, Jews were required to take a special public oath before the town judge and clerk. This oath was not fully abolished until a century later.

Jews received Danish citizenship in 1814, and all restrictive legislation against them was abolished by mid-century. The Jewish population increased steadily until the middle of the nineteenth century, when there were approximately 4,200 Jews in Denmark. In the early twentieth century, several hundred refugees from the Eastern European pogroms settled permanently in Denmark.

On April 9, 1940, Germany invaded and occupied Denmark. In the summer of 1943 preparations were made to begin deporting Denmark's Jews. A German diplomat named Georg Ferdinand Duckwitz secretly informed the Danish resistance of the impending danger to the Jews. A rescue organization was immediately established that enabled 7,200 Jews—most of Denmark's Jewish population—to be clandestinely ferried across the Oresund Strait to Sweden. It is unlikely that, as popular myth has it, King Christian X wore a yellow star in solidarity with his Jewish subjects, but he spoke out against the Nazi occupation and the oppression of the Jews. In 1941, after an arson attack at a synagogue in Copenhagen, he sent a letter of sympathy to Rabbi Marcus Melchior. Of the approximately 500 Danish Jews sent by the Nazis to Theresienstadt, almost ninety percent survived the war, largely because of pressure brought to bear by the Danish government on the Germans.

There are about 7,000 Jews living in Denmark today, and the country maintains warm and supportive relations with Israel.

Dutch

Bedikat Hametz: A family searches for leaven on the night before Passover.
A woodcut from *Sefer Ha-Minhagim* (The Book of Customs),
published in Amsterdam in 1662.

*(Jerusalem, Jewish National and University Library. Photo courtesy of
Beth Hatefutsoth Photo Archive, Tel Aviv)*

Wat is het verschil tussen deze avond en alle
andere avonden?

Op alle andere avonden eten we brood met gist en brood zonder gist;
waarom vanavond alleen brood zonder gist?

Alle andere avonden eten we allerlei groenten;
waarom vanavond alleen bitter kruid?

Alle andere avonden dopen we niet in, zelfs niet een keer;
waarom dopen we vanavond twee maal in?

Alle andere avonden eten we rechtop zittend of leunend;
waarom leunen we vanavond allemaal?

THE JEWS OF THE NETHERLANDS

T HE REGION now consisting of the Netherlands, Belgium, and Luxembourg was known as the "Low Countries" in Roman times, which was when the first Jews probably arrived. Little is known about this community until the thirteenth and fourteenth centuries. After the Black Plague in 1349–50, most of the Jews were either massacred or expelled, because it was erroneously believed that they had caused the pandemic.

The seventeenth century witnessed the arrival from Portugal of many secret Jews (known as *conversos* or Marranos), descendants of Jews who had been expelled from Spain in 1492. These Jews formed a Sephardic community in Amsterdam, where they contributed to a general cultural golden age. Unlike their poorer Ashkenazic counterparts, they were prominent in business and medicine, and in the diamond industry. But the community was often rocked by religious controversy. In 1656, the philosopher Baruch Spinoza was excommunicated by the Jewish community for his heretical views.

The political and economic status of the Netherlands and of its Jewish inhabitants declined significantly in the seventeenth and eighteenth centuries, when the Dutch Republic was overshadowed by the expanding power of Great Britain at sea and France on land. By the end of the eighteenth century, more than half of the Jewish population was living off charity. Jews began to lobby for emancipation, which was officially granted to them in 1796.

In 1814, the kingdom of the Netherlands was established as an independent country. King William I instituted compulsory secular education and waged a battle against Yiddish, which resulted in the Jews' widespread adoption of Dutch. But the economic status of the Jews began to improve only in the second half of the century, as Jews moved to the cities and began to gain access to the professional classes.

In 1939–40, thousands of refugees from Nazi Germany arrived in the Netherlands. But then the Nazis invaded and occupied the Netherlands and began to deport its Jews to concentration camps. The only Jews who were able to remain were those who forged their identity papers or went into hiding—including, most famously, Anne Frank and her family, who hid with the assistance of non-Jews but were eventually betrayed by unknown persons. By the end of the war, only 25 percent of the prewar Jewish population of 140,000 had survived. Sixty years later, in April 2005, Holland's prime minister Jan Peter Balkenende apologized for his country's collaboration with the Nazis.

There are approximately 40,000 Jews in the Netherlands today.

Farsi

These Iranian girls at their Bat Mitzvah celebration are required by Islamic law to cover their hair in public. Note the pictures of the late Ayatollah Khomeini and former president Akbar Hashemi Rafsanjani, prominently displayed on the walls in this Jewish community center in Tehran, ca. 1990.

(Courtesy of Rahmat Rahimian)

Cherah een shab ba'ah shab hayeh deegar
fargh dareht?

Dar shab hayeh deegar mah ya na'an ya fateer meekhoreem;
valley em shab faghat fateer meekhoreem.

Dar shab hayeh deegar hameh jour sabzie meekhoreem;
valley em shab faghat sabzeyeh talkh meekhoreem.

Dar shab hayeh deegar mah sabzeeh-ra dar cirqueh hatah
yek bar haleem nemizaneem; valley em shab dough
bar meezaneem.

Dar shab hayeh deegar mah ghazayeh-mon rah hajourey
khosteem meekhoreem; valley em shab kaj meesheeneem vah
meekhoreem.

چقدر فرق دارد امشب با تمام شبهای دیگر. که در سایر شبها ما سبزی یاکاهو را حتی یکدفعه هم در سرکه یا حلق نمیزنیم ولی امشب این کار را دربار انجام میدهیم.

در شبهای دیگر ما ازنان تخمیر شده یا فطیر میخوریم ولی امشب همه را فقط نان فطیر صرف میکنیم. در شبهای دیگر ما سایر سبزیجات را میخوریم ولی امشب ار سبزی تلح اسلفاده میکنیم. درشبهای دیگر دیگر ما خواه در حال نشسته و خواء در حال تکیه دادن بر روی آرنج چپ میخوریم ومینوشیم ولی امشب همه ما در موقع نوشیدن یائین یا خوردن مصا بر روی آرنج چپ تکیه میدهیم.

دو اینموقع سینی پسح را سرمیز بر گردانیده و بقیه هگادا را میخوانیم. در موقع خواندن هگادا بایستی روی سه مصا باز باشد. و فقط در موقعی که پیاله یائین را در دست میگیریم روی سه مصا را می پو شانیم.

بزرك خانوده جواب میدهد.

THE JEWS OF PERSIA

THE PERSIAN JEWISH community includes the Jews of Iran, as well as those living in parts of Afghanistan, Pakistan, Uzbekistan, and other neighboring countries. In 538 B.C.E., the Persian ruler Cyrus the Great conquered Babylon and permitted the Jews, who had been expelled from the Kingdom of Judah by the Babylonian ruler Nebuchadnezzar, to return to Israel, though many chose to remain in exile.

The books of Daniel, Ezra, Ezekiel, and Esther describe Jewish life in the Persian Empire, where the Jews enjoyed religious and economic freedom. But the Muslim Arab conquest of Persia in the seventh century led to a change in their situation. Jews were forced to wear yellow ribbons on their arms to distinguish them from Muslims, and a heavy tax was imposed upon them.

In the thirteenth century, the situation of the Jews improved when the Mongols conquered the Persian Empire. But this changed in the sixteenth and seventeenth centuries, under the Safawid dynasty, when the form of Islam known as Shiism became the state religion. Those Jews who refused to convert were considered ritually unclean and had to wear special headgear as a sign of their inferior status. Finally, in 1661, the Persian authorities issued an edict allowing the Jews to return to their religious worship.

Under the Kajar dynasty (1794–1925) Jews were once again persecuted until, in 1908, a constitution granted equal rights to Christians, Jews, and Zoroastrians, the three minority religions. At the beginning of the twentieth century, as part of a campaign by European Jews, the first Jewish schools were opened in Persia. As interest in the Zionist movement spread through the Persian Jewish community, many Jews left for Palestine.

In 1925, Reza Khan Pahlavi was crowned shah. He carried out far-reaching reforms, including the political emancipation of the Jews. But his regime was also known for ruthless suppression of dissent, and in 1979 the shah was overthrown and the Muslim cleric Ayatollah Khomeini established an Islamic republic. In his speeches he attacked Israel, Zionism, and world Jewry. In response to harsh political conditions in the new republic, Jewish emigration turned into a mass exodus, and the population of Jews in Iran dropped significantly. There are currently approximately 30,000 Jews in Iran.

French

"The Great Sanhedrin of the Jews of France." In 1806, Napoleon Bonaparte invited seventy-one rabbis to re-create the Jewish Supreme Court of ancient Israel, to answer twelve questions about the religious practices of the newly emancipated Jews. The Sanhedrin held several public meetings, published replies to the questions, and then disbanded. This is a fictional depiction of one of the sessions. Lithograph by Vernier after E. Moyse, 1868.

(Beth Hatefutsoth Photo Archive, Tel Aviv. Courtesy of Iona Hasmias, Tel Aviv)

Pourquoi cette nuit se distingue-t-elle de toutes les autres nuits?

Toutes les autres nuits, il nous est permis de manger du pain au levain comme du pain azyme; cette nuit seulement du pain azyme.

Toutes les autres nuits nous mangeons des herbes quelconques; cette nuit que des herbes amères.

Toutes les autres nuits, nous ne trempons pas (les aliments) même une seule fois et; cette nuit nous les trempons deux fois.

Toutes les autres nuits, nous mangeons et buvons assis ou allongés; cette nuit nous sommes tous allongés.

THE JEWS OF FRANCE

J EWS HAVE BEEN living in France since 465 C.E. By the time of the emperor Charlemagne (742–814), the Jewish community had grown significantly due to immigration from Spain and Italy. Jews were granted legal equality and were actively involved in commercial affairs. A rich Jewish intellectual culture developed and reached its climax in the eleventh century with the biblical and Talmudic commentaries of Rabbi Solomon ben Isaac, better known by the acronym of his name, Rashi (1040–1105), who was born in Troyes and is considered by many to be the greatest rabbinic commentator in Jewish history.

In 1096, the First Crusade, which was a call by Pope Urban II to liberate the Holy Land from its Muslim rulers, led to centuries of persecution of Europe's Jews, who were accused of using the blood of murdered Christians in their ritual practices. The Jews of France were also subject to repeated expulsions, most famously in 1306 and 1394. Beginning in 1550, Jews who had been expelled from Spain and Portugal were granted permission to resettle in France, although they were forced to pay severe taxes.

In the eighteenth century, the French government became more tolerant toward the Jews. In 1791, two years after the outbreak of the French Revolution, the French National Assembly granted them full citizenship. Napoleon Bonaparte spread the idea of political emancipation of the Jews throughout all of the European countries that he conquered. In 1807, he made Judaism one of the official religions of France. But the scourge of anti-Semitism was never completely eliminated. In 1894, a Jewish officer in the French army named Alfred Dreyfus was falsely accused of treason, convicted, and sentenced to life in prison on Devil's Island. The writer Émile Zola, in an open letter to the president of France that was published in a newspaper in 1898, brought the injustice of Dreyfus's treatment to public attention. Dreyfus was eventually pardoned and, later, exonerated, but the Dreyfus Affair continued to divide the nation.

By the early part of the nineteenth century, many Jews became prominent cultural figures, including the artists Marc Chagall and Amedeo Modigliani. France was also the first country to elect a Jewish prime minister, Léon Blum, in 1936.

Germany invaded and conquered France in 1940. France's Jews were deported to concentration camps; 25 percent of France's prewar population of 300,000 was murdered in the Holocaust.

The postwar French-Jewish population nearly doubled in the second half of the twentieth century with the arrival first of European Jewish war refugees and, later, Sephardic Jews from the French colonies in North Africa. There are currently approximately 600,000 Jews in France.

German

Bedikat Hametz: A family searches for leaven on the night before Passover.
Postcard reproducing a painting by Hermann Junker, Frankfurt am Main,
Germany, from the end of the nineteenth century.

Was zeichnet diese Nacht vor
allen anderen Nächten aus?

In allen anderen Nächten essen wir gesäuertes und ungesäuertes Brot; in dieser Nacht nur Mazza.

In allen anderen Nächten essen wir die verschiedensten Kräuter; in dieser Nacht nur Bitterkraut (Maror).

In allen anderen Nächten tunken wir gar nicht ein; in dieser Nacht zweimal.

In allen anderen Nächten essen wir entweder frei sitzend oder angelehnt; in dieser Nacht nur angelehnt.

THE JEWS OF GERMANY

JEWS BEGAN LIVING in Germany in the early Middle Ages, when Jewish merchants arrived from southern Italy and France. By the end of the tenth century, the cities of Mainz and Worms became spiritual centers that attracted many scholars, including the famous French biblical and talmudic commentator known as Rashi.

Persecution of the Jews in Germany began in 1096 with the First Crusade, which started as a call by Pope Urban II to the Christians of Europe to liberate the Holy Land from its Muslim rulers. The Crusades resulted in terrible persecution of Europe's Jews. They were forced out of their trades, and many had no choice but to become moneylenders, an activity that was forbidden to Christians. But they nonetheless maintained an intense spiritual life: Jewish scholars wrote great works of religious law and poetry during this time.

The situation improved in the sixteenth and seventeenth centuries, when a new form of government known as enlightened absolutism resulted in greater respect for those Jews with economic expertise. At the end of the eighteenth century, in response to the major strides made in the secular world in the arts and sciences and in the study of philosophy, many Jews sought more modern approaches to the practice of Judaism, as opposed to traditional religious ones. This movement was known as the Haskalah, or Enlightenment, and was best exemplified in the writings of the philosopher Moses Mendelssohn. The first decades of the nineteenth century witnessed the rise of what later became known as Reform Judaism, with its emphasis on ethical practices rather than strict adherence to Jewish law and ritual. Jews attained political and civil equality and, for the most part, enjoyed a period of general prosperity until the Nazis seized power in 1933.

In 1935, the German government adopted the Nuremberg Laws, which defined Judaism in terms of race and denied citizenship to all Jews. More than 300,000 Jews fled the country between 1933 and 1939 in response to Nazi persecution. As European countries fell before the German army beginning in 1939, the Jews of these countries were rounded up and killed en masse or deported first to ghettos and then to concentration camps, where they were murdered or forced to become slave laborers. The "Final Solution of the Jewish Question," as outlined in a secret conference held by top Nazi officials in January 1942, was to be the annihilation of all of Europe's Jews. For many years after World War II, the Jewish community in Germany consisted mostly of a few hundred Holocaust survivors. But in the 1980s Jews began to arrive from the former Soviet Union, revitalizing the Jewish community. Holocaust denial in Germany is now a criminal act that can be punishable with imprisonment.

There are approximately 200,000 Jews living in Germany today.

Greek

A scene from the play *La Mujer Desconosida* (The Unknown Woman),
performed by members of the Jewish Amateur Theater in Salonika,
Greece, in 1930.

(Beth Hatefutsoth Photo Archive, Tel Aviv. Courtesy of Flora Safan-Eskaloni)

To ékplikto pedí pu káthete dípla ston patéra
ke kamaróni sto trapézi tin ómorfi mitéra
rotá na máthi yiatí in᾽ i níhta aftí xehoristí
k᾽ ap᾽ óles tis álles tóso diafotretikí?

Yiatí apópse ázimo vlépi s᾽ aláti vutigméno;
enó tes álles tes vradiés to psomí ᾽ne zimoméno?

Yiatí óli ti hroniá káthe logís tróme vlastári;
enó apópse idiétera éna pikró hortári?

Yiatí kathimerís adiáfora tróme kathisméni;
enó etúti ti vradiá se polithrónes throniasméni?

Τὸ ἔκπληκτο παιδὶ ποὺ κάθεται δίπλα στὸν πατέρα
Καὶ καμαρώνει στὸ τραπέζι τὴν ὄμορφη μητέρα
Ρωτᾶ νὰ μάθη γιατὶ εἶν' ἡ νύχτα αὐτὴ ξεχωριστὴ
Κ' ἀπ' ὅλες τὶς ἄλλες νύχτες τόσο διαφορετική;

Γιατὶ ἀπόψε ἄζυμο βλέπει σ' ἁλάτι βουτηγμένο
Ἐνῶ τὲς ἄλλες τὲς βραδυὲς τὸ ψωμί 'ναι ζυμωμένο;

Γιατὶ ὅλη τή χρονιὰ κάθε λογῆς τρῶμε βλαστάρι,
Ἐνῶ ἀπόψε ἰδιαίτερα ἕνα πικρὸ χορτάρι;*

Γιατὶ καθημερὶς ἀδιάφορα τρῶμε καθισμένοι,
Ἐνῶ ἐτούτη τὴ βραδυὰ σὲ πολυθρόνες θρονιασμένοι.

*Not appearing in this version is the question about the two dippings.

THE JEWS OF GREECE

THE FIRST EVIDENCE of a Jewish presence in Greece dates back to the third century B.C.E., although Jews may have been forcibly transported there as slaves during biblical times. After the conquest of the Persian Empire (which included ancient Israel) by Alexander the Great, many Jews under Greek rule adopted the Greek language and aspects of Hellenistic culture.

The most significant confrontation between the Jews of ancient Israel and the Greeks was the Maccabean Revolt (167–164 B.C.E.), which we celebrate today with the festival of Chanukah. The revolt resulted in the establishment of a Jewish government led by the Hasmoneans, and many Hellenized Jews left to settle in Greece. Greece fell to the Roman Empire in 146 B.C.E., and Jews living in Greece became known as "Romaniot," or Jews of the "second Rome." They translated prayers into Greek, which were then recorded in Hebrew letters.

Jews lived in Greece continuously throughout the Byzantine period (330–1453). They were granted legal and economic protection, but this did not prevent them from being subjected to several forced conversions, particularly before the eleventh century. Over time, several Jewish communities became associated with particular industries, such as silk spinning.

In 1453, Greece became part of the Ottoman Empire, which lasted until the early part of the twentieth century. Throughout this period, the center of Jewish life was Thessaloniki (Salonika). The Ladino-speaking Sephardic Jews of Salonika, thousands of whom had arrived after the expulsion from Spain in 1492, established the city's first printing press and were active in commerce and trade.

During the Greek War of Independence (1821–32), thousands of Jews were massacred by their Christian Orthodox neighbors, and several communities were destroyed. The situation improved in midcentury, and, in 1912, Ottoman rule came to an end. The newly established Greek government won the support of the Jewish community.

Greece was occupied by the Axis powers during World War II. More than 12,000 Jews fought in the Greek army, first against the Italians and then against the Germans. More than 60,000 Jews—approximately 85 percent of the Jewish population—were killed during the war, despite efforts by the Greek Orthodox Church hierarchy and many individual Christian Greeks to hide Jews.

There are approximately 5,500 Jews living in Greece today, the majority of them in Athens, where the first kosher restaurant since World War II was opened in July 2004 to serve Jewish athletes arriving for the 2004 Summer Olympics.

Hungarian

This depiction of one of the two hand-washing rituals of the seder was painted onto a seder plate that was manufactured by the Jewish-owned Herend Porcelain Factory, in Herend, Hungary, ca. 1850.

(Beth Hatefutsoth Photo Archive, Tel Aviv)

Miert ish oyan mash ez az ayel minden mash ayelnel?*

Minden mash ayelen ehetunk kovasochat meg kovastolant;
ezen az ayelen chukish kovastolant.

Minden mash ayelen ehetunk barmefeiteh zuldcheget;
ezen az ayelen kesherut kel enyunk.

Minden mash ayelen nem kel bemartenyunk etzer shem;
ezen az ayelen kaytzer ish.

Minden mash ehetunk akar edyuneshen alvah akar tamuzkodvo;
ezen az ayelen mindyanyunk chuk tamuzkodvo.

*transliteration

Miért is olyan más ez az éjjel minden más éjjelnél?

Minden más éjjelen ehetünk kovászosat meg kovásztalant;
ezen az éjjelen csakis kovásztalant.

Minden más éjjelen ehetünk bármiféle zöldséget;
ezen az éjjelen keserüt kell ennünk.

Minden más éjjelen nem kell bemártanunk egyszer sem;
ezen az éjjelen kétszer is.

Minden más éjjelen ehetünk akár egyenesen ülve, akár támaszkodva;
ezen az éjjelen mindnyájunk csak támaszkodva.

J EWS HAVE BEEN living in Hungary since the time of the Roman Empire. The Jewish community began to grow significantly in the eleventh century, when immigrants arrived from Germany, Bohemia, and Moravia. The Christian Church imposed several restrictions on the Jews: They were forbidden to intermarry, work on Sundays and Christian festivals, and purchase slaves. But the Hungarian kings supported and protected the Jews and granted them legal rights.

In 1541, Hungary became part of the Ottoman Empire. Under Ottoman rule, Jews were allowed to practice their religion and participate in economic life. But the situation deteriorated in the late seventeenth century, when Hungary became part of the Habsburg Empire. The Jews were forced to pay "tolerance taxes" and were subject to widespread persecution.

In the early part of the nineteenth century, the majority of Hungarian Jews were religiously Orthodox. They were led by Moses Sofer of Pressburg (the Hatam Sofer), who promoted Torah study and Zionism. In 1867, the Jews of Hungary were granted political emancipation. The Jewish population grew tremendously, and Jews became active in agriculture, business, finance, and the arts. They also began to intermarry and assimilate into the general population.

Following World War I, in which more than 10,000 Hungarian Jews lost their lives, the communists took control and Jews became involved in the government. But in 1919, the Austro-Soviet republic was dissolved and more than 3,000 Jews were killed in a massacre known as the "White Terror." Anti-Jewish legislation barred many Jews from their former workplaces, and the situation deteriorated even further when Hungary joined the Axis powers during World War II. In 1944, Germany occupied Hungary, and Jews were deported to ghettos and concentration camps. Several thousand Jews were saved through the efforts of individuals such as Hannah Senesh, a Jewish resistance fighter who had immigrated to Palestine, and Raoul Wallenberg, the secretary of the Swedish Legation in Budapest. But only 260,000 out of a prewar population of 825,000 Hungarian Jews survived the war.

From 1949 to 1989, the communists ruled Hungary. They banned Zionist activities and expelled many Jews from the cities to the provinces. Despite persistent anti-Semitism and assimilation, Budapest is now home to a Jewish museum and three Jewish schools, as well as several cultural and religious centers in other major Hungarian cities. Approximately 100,000 Jews live in Hungary today.

Italian

This etching of the Piazza Giudia (The Square of the Jews) is the work of
the eighteenth-century engraver and architect Giuseppe Vasi.
On the right a doorway is visible. From 1555 to 1870 the door was
closed every evening by Roman police, locking the Jews of Rome
into their infamous ghetto.

(Beth Hatefutsoth Photo Archive, Tel Aviv. Courtesy of Roberto Milano, Rome)

Che differenza c'è fra questa e tutte le altre notti?

Perchè tutte le altre notti possiamo mangiare
pane lievitato e azzimo; e questa notte soltanto
azzimo.

Perchè tutte le altre notti possiamo mangiare
ogni tipo di verdura; e questa notte l'erba amara.

Perchè tutte le altre notti non possiamo intingere
nemmeno una volta; e questa notte dobbiamo
intingere due volte.

Perchè tutte le altre notti noi mangiamo e
beviamo o seduti o appoggiati col gomito; e
questa notte siamo tutti appoggiati col gomito.

THE JEWS OF ITALY

ITALY IS HOME to the oldest Jewish community in Europe, dating back two thousand years. The first Jews were sent as envoys to Rome from Palestine by the Hasmonean ruler Judah Maccabee in 161 B.C.E. Jews were generally tolerated in ancient Rome, although the Roman Empire's official acceptance of Christianity in 313 C.E. made their lives more difficult. In the early Middle Ages, new laws barred the Jews from serving in the government and building new synagogues, so medieval Italian Jews worked as farmers and merchants. They established Talmudic academies in Rome and in several southern cities.

The years 1300 to 1500 marked the high point of Jewish life in Italy. Jews began working as moneylenders, which led to widespread prosperity. The Soncino family, immigrants from Alsatia, established one of the world's first Hebrew printing presses in 1484, which produced the first printed copies of the Bible, the Siddur (prayer book), and tractates of the Talmud. But this period of great cultural activity came to an abrupt end in 1492, when almost 40,000 Jews in Sicily and Sardinia were forced to flee the country. In the mid-sixteenth century, the Jews of northern and central Italy were confined to ghettos and isolated from the outside world.

Italian Jews began to gain freedom and equality in the nineteenth century, when the country experienced waves of revolutionary activity.

In 1848, Pope Pius IX ordered that the walls of the ghetto in Rome be demolished. That same year, Piedmont, which soon expanded to become the kingdom of Italy, established equal civil and political rights for all its citizens. The Jews seized the opportunity to embrace new careers, gaining positions of power and prestige.

In 1922, Benito Mussolini came to power, but it was not until 1937 that the fascist government became militantly anti-Semitic. In 1943, Mussolini surrendered to Hitler, and the Jews of Italy came under Nazi rule. Jews were interned in concentration camps and their property was confiscated; by the end of the war, more than one-fifth of the Jewish population had been decimated.

After World War II, the Jews of Italy established two rabbinical seminaries and a system of Jewish schools. Italy was also one of the first countries to establish diplomatic relations with the State of Israel. There are approximately 40,000 Jews living in Italy today.

Ladino

שָׁם לְגוֹי גָּדוֹל וְעָצוּם כְּמוֹ שֶׁנֶּאֱמַר וּבְנֵי יִשְׂרָאֵל פָּרוּ וַיִּשְׁרְצוּ
וַיִּרְבּוּ וַיַּעַצְמוּ בִּמְאֹד מְאֹד וַתִּמָּלֵא הָאָרֶץ אוֹתָם:
וָרָב כְּמָה שֶׁנֶּאֱמַר רְבָבָה כְּצֶמַח הַשָּׂדֶה נְתַתִּיךְ
וַתִּרְבִּי

אֵלֵי פ֞וֹרְגֵ֞ינֵ֞יטֵ֞י גְ֞רַאנְדֵ֞י אִי פֿוּאֵ֞רְטֵ֞י ׳וְקִ֞ימוֹ דִ֞יזֵ֞י אִיל פָּסוּק אִי י֞אַנוֹש דֵ֞י יִשְׂרָאֵל פֿרוֹנִי֞ינוֹארוֹן
אִי מוֹנְ֞י֞יגוֹ֞ארוֹנְסֵ֞י אִי אֵ֞נפֿוֹרְטֵ֞יסֵ֞ירֵ֞ינַסִי אֵ֞ן רוֹ מוּגוֹ מוּגוֹ אִי אִינ֞ינוֹסֵ֞י לַה סִ֞ייֵ֞רַה דֵ֞י אֵ֞לְיוֹש
וְרָב אִי ׳מוּגוֹ קוֹמוֹ׃ דִ֞יזֵ֞י אִיל פָּסוּק מִילְ׳אַרְי֞יַא קוֹמוֹ אִירְ׳מוֹלְ֞י֞ירוֹ דֵ֞ל ׳׳׳׳׳ דֵ֞י דֵ֞י

This woodcut is from the Livorno Haggadah, which was printed in 1825 in Italy and contains dozens of illustrations. The drawing of European-looking women who are rather overwhelmed with children illustrates the passage in the Haggadah that tells us that the Israelites in Pharoh's Egypt "were fruitful, and increased, and multiplied, and became strong." Beneath the Hebrew text is the Ladino text in Hebrew characters.

Kuanto fue demud'ad'a la noçe la esta,
mas ke tod'as las noçes?

Ke en tod'as las noçes, nos komientes chametz o
matzah; i la noçe la esta tod'o el matzah.

Ke en tod'as las noçes nos komientes resto de ved'ruras;
i la noçe la esta liçuga.

Ke en tod'as las noçes, non nos entinientes afilu ves una;
i la noçe la esta dos vezes.

Ke en tod'as las noçes, nos komientes i bevientes,
keen asentad'os i keen areskovdad'os; i la noçe la esta
tod'os nos areskovdad'os.

קוּאַנְטוֹ פ'וּאִי דֵּימוּדָאדָה לָה נוֹגֵ'י לָה אִיסְטָה מָאס
קֵי טוֹדָאס לָאס נוֹגֵ'יס?

קֵי אֵין טוֹדָאס לָאס נוֹגֵ'יס נוֹס קוֹמְיֵינְטֵיס חָמֵץ אוֹ מַצָה;
אִי לָה נוֹגֵ'י לָה אִיסְטָה: טוֹדוּ אֵיל מַצָה.

קֵי אֵין טוֹדָאס לַאס נוֹגֵ'יס נוֹס קוֹמְיֵינְטֵיס רֵיסְטוֹ דֵּי וְיִדְרוּרָאס;
אִי לָה נוֹגֵ'י לָה אִיסְטָה: לִיגֵ'וּגָה.

קֵי אֵין טוֹדָאס לָאס נוֹגֵ'יס נוֹן נוֹס אֵינְטִיןֵינְטֵיס אַפ'ִילוּ בֵּ'יס אוּנָה;
אִי לָה נוֹגֵ'י לָה אִיסְטָה: דוֹס בֵּ'יזֵיס.

קֵי אֵין טוֹדָאס לָאס נוֹגֵ'יס נוֹס קוֹמְיֵינְטֵיס אִי בִּיבֵ'יֵנְטֵיס
קוֹן אַסִינְטָאדוֹס אִי קֵיֵין אַרֵיסְקוֹבֵ'דָאדוֹס; אִי לָה נוֹגֵ'י לָה:
אִיסְטָה טוֹדוֹס נוֹס אַרֵיסְקוֹבֵ'דָאדוֹס.

L ADINO, ALSO KNOWN AS Judeo-Spanish, Sefardi, Judezmo, and Spanyol, is a language spoken by Jews of Spanish origin (Sephardim). It began as the language of the general population in Castilian Spain in the Middle Ages and became a specifically Jewish language after the Jews were expelled from Spain in 1492. These Jews were cut off from the further development of Castilian Spanish, but they continued to speak the ancient form of it in the countries to which they immigrated. This is why Ladino is linguistically similar to modern Spanish, but also has many terms from Hebrew, Arabic, Portuguese, French, Turkish, Greek, and Slavic languages, depending on where the speakers reside.

The two main dialects of Ladino are Oriental and Western. Oriental Ladino was spoken in Turkey and Rhodes, and reflected Castilian Spanish; Western Ladino was spoken in Greece, Macedonia, Bulgaria, Bosnia, Serbia, and Romania, and preserved the characteristics of northern Spanish and Portuguese.

Ladino is a written language as well as a spoken one. The earliest Ladino literature was limited to translations from Hebrew. At the end of the seventeenth century, Ladino began to replace Hebrew as the vehicle for rabbinic instruction. One of the most famous Ladino works is *Me'am Lo'ez,* an anthology of rabbinic literature written by Rabbi

Yaakov Culi (1685–1732) and intended for general use by all Jews. Over time, new secular genres appeared in Ladino as well, including poetry, history, biography, drama, and journals. The Nobel Prize–winning author Elias Canetti was born into a Ladino-speaking Sephardic family in Bulgaria in 1905.

In the nineteenth century, Ladino was written in Hebrew characters. Today, the language is most commonly written in the Latin alphabet.

The Nazis destroyed most of the communities in Europe, such as Salonika, where Ladino had been the primary Jewish language. Ladino speakers who survived the Holocaust and emigrated to Latin America tended to pick up contemporary Spanish very quickly, while others adopted the language of their new homelands. Today, there are a little more than 100,000 Ladino-speaking Jews throughout the world; the greatest number of them live in Israel and Turkey.

Latin

This relief carved into the Arch of Titus, located in the Roman Forum, shows a triumphal procession of soldiers carrying through the streets of Rome sacred items taken from the Temple in Jerusalem. The arch was erected by the emperor Domitian about ten years after the death of his brother, the emperor Titus, during whose reign the Temple was destroyed in 70 C.E.

(Beth Hatefutsoth Photo Archive, Permanent Exhibition, Tel Aviv)

Quo differt haec nox a ceteris noctibus?

Quod ceteris noctibus et fermentum et azymum comedimus;
hac nocte autem solum azymum.

Quod ceteris noctibus omnia olera comedimus;
hac nocte autem lactucam.

Quod ceteris noctibus ne semel quidem intingimus;
hac nocte autem bis.

Quod ceteris noctibus comedentes vel sedemus vel recumbimus;
hac nocte autem omnes recumbimus.

THE JEWS OF ANCIENT ROME

L ATIN WAS ONE of the languages spoken in ancient Rome. Jews first settled there in the time of the Maccabees (about 161 B.C.E.), but the Jewish population began to grow significantly only after the Romans invaded Judea in 63 B.C.E. In 70 C.E. the Romans destroyed the Temple in Jerusalem, and about fifteen hundred Jews were brought back to Rome as slaves and prisoners of war.

By the second half of the first century C.E., the Jewish community in Rome was firmly established with a population of about twenty-five thousand. Most Jews worked as shopkeepers and craftsmen, though there were also Jewish beggars, physicians, actors, and poets. About twelve synagogues were built during this period, though none remain standing today. In about 75 C.E., the controversial Jewish historian Flavius Josephus published *The Jewish War,* the only contemporary account of the revolt of the Jews against the Romans, which ended in the destruction of the second Temple and the exile of most of the Jewish population of Palestine.

Throughout the second and third centuries, the Jews of Rome were generally treated benevolently by the Roman government. They do not seem to have been significantly affected by the Bar Kokhba Revolt, a heroic but failed uprising led by a Judean leader against the Roman emperor Hadrian in 132–35 C.E. The Jews of Rome became full citizens in 212 C.E., along with all the other free men in the empire. But the Roman Empire's official acceptance of Christianity in 313 C.E. made their lives more difficult.

Most Jews living in ancient Rome spoke not Latin but Greek, as ancient tombstone inscriptions attest. Latin words figure much less frequently in rabbinic literature than Greek ones, and the rabbis generally ignored Latin literature. Nonetheless, Roman court procedures influenced the shaping of Jewish law: A Jewish bill of divorce, for instance, would be invalidated if it did not contain the proper Roman date. The Talmud includes many dialogues among the rabbis about the value of Roman law and culture; opinions range from praise for the Roman system of justice to harsh warnings against adopting the Roman style of dress.

Marathi

These Hindu women are in the courtyard of the Magen David synagogue in Bombay, preparing Passover matzah for the entire Jewish community of Bombay, ca. 1979.

(Carmel Berkson, Bombay. Beth Hatefutsoth Photo Archive, Tel Aviv.
Carmel Berkson Collection, Bombay)

Sarva ratrihoon hi ratra bhinna ka?

Sarva ratris kontahi padartha ek vel hi budwoon khath nahi;
hya ratris don vela budwoon khato.

Sarva ratris khamir ani bekhmir bharkar khato;
parantu hya ratris keval bekhmir bharker khato.

Sarva ratris sarva prakarchi hirvat bhaji khato;
hya ratris kadvat bhaji matra khato.

Sarva ratris basun athva takun khato ani pito;
ani hya ratris apan sarva lok dave bajus takun khato ani pito.

सर्व रात्रीहून ही रात्र भिन्न कां?

सर्व रात्रीस कोणताही पदार्थ एक वेळ ही बुडवून खात नाही; ह्या रात्रीस दोन वेळा बुडवून खातो.

सर्व रात्रीस खमीर आणि बेखमीर भाकर खातो; परंतु ह्या रात्रीस केवळ बेखमीर भाकर खातो.

सर्व रात्रीस सर्व प्रकारची हिरवट भाजी खातो; ह्या रात्रीस कडवट भाजी मात्र खातो.

सर्व रात्रीस बसून अथवा टेकून खातो आणि पितो; आणि ह्या रात्रीस आपण सर्व लोक डावे बाजूस टेकून खातो व पितो.

THE JEWS OF INDIA

MARATHI IS THE Indian language spoken by the Bene Israel, the Indian Jewish community that lived for centuries on the Konkan (southwestern) coast of the Indian subcontinent, and subsequently established communities in Bombay, Calcutta, Old Delhi, and Ahmadabad. The Bene Israel are the oldest Jewish community in India, and some scholars claim that they are descended from one of the ten "lost" tribes of the kingdom of Israel, sent into exile by the Assyrians in the eighth century B.C.E. But the first historical evidence of a Bene Israel presence in India is not until the early eleventh century.

In the eighteenth century, the Bene Israel were "discovered" by Jewish traders from Baghdad. At that time the only forms of Jewish practice they knew about were circumcision, kashrut, the observance of Shabbat, and the prohibition against intermarriage. There were 6,000 Bene Israel in the mid-1800s and 10,000 at the turn of the twentieth century. In 1948, they numbered 20,000, but with the establishment of the State of Israel many Bene Israel made aliyah, despite the fact that they had never experienced significant persecution from their Hindu and Muslim neighbors. There are about 4,000 Bene Israel living in India today. In 1964, the Israeli Rabbinate declared that the Bene Israel are "full Jews in every respect." And in 2002, DNA testing confirmed that the Bene Israel share the same heredity as the Israelite priestly class, from whom they have long claimed descent.

There are two other Jewish communities in India. The Jews of Cochin, who speak the Indian language Malayalam, have lived on the Malabar (southern) coast for centuries—some claim since the time of King Solomon. Others say they arrived in the first century C.E., following the destruction of the Temple. They had their own principality for many centuries until an internal dispute led neighboring princes to dispossess them. Today, most of this community, like the Bene Israel, has emigrated to Israel. The "Baghdadi" Jews immigrated to India during the time of the British rule, chiefly from Iraq but from other Middle Eastern countries as well. They have largely assimilated into Indian society.

Polish

These men are carrying a can in which the Jews in their neighborhood could
kasher their pots, pans, and utensils for Passover. The photograph was taken
in Łódz´, Poland, during World War I, by a soldier in the German army.

(Beth Hatefutsoth Photo Archive, Tel Aviv. Gringras Collection)

Tchemo ruzhni shen notz ta od vzhystkichy in nich notze?*

Bo vzhiski in ne notze spozhevame kizhone lop nikezhone;
notze te zash tilko nikezhone.

Bo vzhiski in ne notze spozhevame rozhne shoa;
notze te tilko gorzhke.

Bo vzhiski in ne notze matchame pokarmov ani raz yeden;
notze te zash dua raze.

Bo vzhiski in ne notze yadame shedzons lop operayons shem;
notze te zash tilko operayons shem.

*transliteration

Czemu różni się noc ta od wszystkich
innych nocy?

Po wszystkie inne noce spożywamy kiszone lub niekiszone;
nocy tej zaś tylko niekiszone.

Po wszystkie inne noce spożywamy różne zioła;
nocy tej tylko gorzkie.

Po wszystkie inne noce nie maczamy pokarmów ani raz jeden;
nocy tej zaś dwa razy.

Po wszystkie inne noce jadamy siedząc lub opierając się;
nocy tej zaś tylko opierając się.

THE JEWS OF POLAND

THE FIRST POLISH JEWS were merchants who arrived from the German Empire in the Middle Ages. In the mid-thirteenth century, they were granted freedom of religion and the right to become moneylenders and businessmen. But their situation deteriorated in the fourteenth century, when they were blamed for the Black Plague and attacked in anti-Semitic riots.

In the late fifteenth and early sixteenth centuries, Jews enjoyed a degree of self-government under an organization known as the Council of Four Lands. By the mid-sixteenth century, Poland was the major center of Ashkenazi Jewry in the world. But the Jews of Poland suffered a devastating blow in the Chmielnicki massacres of 1648–49, in which a Ukrainian army officer led local peasants and Russian Cossacks in an uprising against the Jews, killing between 100,000 and 150,000.

The late seventeenth and early eighteenth centuries witnessed the rise of the religious movement known as Hasidism, with its emphasis on mysticism and religious fervor. The founder of this movement, Rabbi Yisroel ben Eliezer, was known as the Ba'al Shem Tov (Master of the Good Name).

In the late eighteenth century, most of Poland's Jews came under Russian rule. Catherine the Great restricted where Jews could live and where they could do business, and they faced continued anti-Semitism. In 1921, Poland became a sovereign state, a development accompanied by a new wave of terror against the Jews. Nonetheless, by the eve of World War II, the Jews of Poland enjoyed a rich social and cultural life, and they composed the second-largest Jewish community in the world. Notable Polish-Jewish cultural figures of the twentieth century include the Nobel Prize–winning authors I. B. Singer and S. Y. Agnon, the actor and director Joseph Green, and the actress Ida Kaminska.

On September 1, 1939, World War II began with Hitler's invasion of Poland. Once there, the Nazis set up both concentration camps and extermination camps, with the goal of eliminating the entire Jewish population of Europe. There were several Jewish attempts to resist the Nazis, including the unsuccessful Warsaw ghetto uprising of 1942. But by the end of the war, nearly three million Polish Jews had been killed, leaving only eleven percent of the prewar population.

Following the war, Jews were still subject to anti-Semitism, with the government now under Soviet Communist influence. The last mass migration of Jews from Poland took place in 1968–69, after the 1967 Six-Day War, when the Polish government closed down Jewish youth camps, schools, and clubs. In 1977, Poland began to try to improve its image regarding Jewish matters. Partial diplomatic relations were restored with Israel in 1986—the first of the communist bloc countries to take this step—but full diplomatic relations were not restored until 1990, a year after Poland ended its communist rule. Between 5,000 and 10,000 Jews live in Poland today, although many Polish Christians are now discovering that they have Jewish ancestors.

Portuguese

These children are attending a "Model Seder" at the Hebrew School of São Paulo, Brazil, in preparation for Passover, 1984.

(Ana Maria Sarmento Solitunick, Brazil. Beth Hatefutsoth
Photo Archive, Tel Aviv. Courtesy of Ana Maria Sarmento Solitunick, Brazil)

De que maneira esta noite se diferencia de todas as noites?

Todas as outras noites comemos pão que é levedado e que não é levedado, nesta noite comemos apenas matsá, pão não levedado.

Todas as outras noites comemos todos os tipos de ervas; nesta noite apenas aquelas que são amargas.

Todas as outras noites não mergulhamos em molhos o que comemos sequer uma ves; nesta noite o fazemos duas vezes.

Todas as outras noites comemos sentados ou reclinados; nesta noite todos reclinados.

THE JEWS OF BRAZIL

PORTUGUESE IS spoken by the Jews of Brazil, a country whose Jewish history dates back to the discovery of the New World. Many came fleeing the religious persecution that took hold in Portugal when the Inquisition began there in 1497. In 1502, a group of *conversos* (Jews who had ostensibly converted to Christianity) were granted royal permission to colonize Brazil. They established mills and sugar plantations. By 1624, when the Dutch took over portions of the country, Jews composed a significant portion of the population. Under the more tolerant Dutch they began once again to practice Judaism, and, in 1636, they built the first synagogue in the New World in the Dutch city of Recife.

In 1654, the Portuguese defeated the Dutch and ordered all the Jews to convert or leave Brazil within three months. The Jews either fled to places like New York (then known as New Amsterdam) and the Caribbean island of Curaçao, or once again became crypto Jews who practiced in secret. Open Jewish life in Brazil did not resume until 1773, when a Portuguese royal decree put an end to more than a century of persecution.

At the beginning of the twentieth century, European Jews began establishing agricultural settlements in Brazil as an alternative to the harsh conditions in Europe. By the start of World War I there were

7,000 Jews living in Brazil. During the two world wars there were tremendous waves of immigration, bringing the Jewish population to more than 55,000 in 1940. Most of these Jews came from Nazi-dominated Western Europe.

Brazil's Jews were subject to a wave of anti-Semitism between 1938 and 1945, when the government issued a decree prohibiting political activities by foreigners. The two existing Yiddish newspapers had to close down, as did the Zionist organization. The situation improved after the war, when a new constitution was adopted and the establishment of the State of Israel reenergized Jewish communities world-wide.

There are about 100,000 Jews living in Brazil today. There is a thriving Jewish culture that includes publications, television programs, synagogues, schools, museums, and academic institutes devoted to Jewish studies. Jews are successful politically and professionally—they are members of the Senate and Cabinet, and they own several major corporations. The community was shaken in 1992 and 1994 by terrorist bombings of Jewish institutions in neighboring Argentina that are still under investigation. But the Brazilian Jewish community itself has experienced only isolated anti-Semitic incidents. In 2001, the synagogue in Recife was reopened, 347 years after it was closed by the Portuguese.

Romanian

"Die Judengasse in Czernowitz, 1924" an etching by Riccardo Righetti
of the "Jews Street" in the Jewish Quarter of Czernowitz
(which was then part of Romania).

(Beth Hatefutsoth Photo Archive, Tel Aviv. Courtesy of Siegfried Geller, Israel)

Péntrooh che seh deosebeshteh acheasta noapteh deh toateh chelelalte noptsi?*

An toáteh chelelalteh noptsi pootém mankáh bookáteh dospeete shi nédospeete; in acheasta noapteh noomay din chele nedospeete.

An chelelalteh noptsi mankaam deeferíteh legoome; in acheásta noápteh mankáam noomay radachéeni (legoomeh) amáreh.

An chelelalteh noptsi nooh trebuye sa inmooyem aleementeh nichi makar o daata; in acheásta noápteh deh dowa ori.

An chelelalteh noptsi mankaam ashezatsi saaw rezematsi; in acheásta noápteh noomay rezematsi.

*transliteration

Pentru ce se deosebeşte această noapte de celelalte nopţi?

În toate celelalte nopţi putem mînca bucate dospite şi nedospite;
în această noapte numai din cele nedospite.

În celelalte nopţi mîncăm diferite legume;
în această noapte numai rădăcini (legume) amare.

În celelalte nopţi nu trebuie să înmuiem alimente nici măcar odată;
în această noapte de două ori.

În celelalte nopţi mîncăm aşezaţi sau rezemaţi;
în această noapte numai rezemaţi.

THE JEWS OF ROMANIA

J EWS LIVED in the region known today as Romania as early as the second century C.E., when it was a Roman province. But a steady Jewish presence did not develop until the medieval period, when members of the Karaite sect (Jews who rejected the Mishnah and Talmud as legally binding texts) settled around the Black Sea. Waves of immigrants arrived from Hungary in the thirteenth century, from Spain in the sixteenth century, and from Poland in the wake of the pogroms of the seventeenth century. Many of these Jews worked as merchants and craftsmen.

The Jews living in the region of present-day Romania were massacred and terrorized during the Russo-Turkish wars of the late eighteenth and early nineteenth centuries. But in 1821 and 1848, during the revolts against first Ottoman and then Russian rulers, the revolutionaries appealed for Jewish support and proclaimed their civic equality. In 1864, Jews were granted the right to vote in the local government councils, but those who were foreign subjects could still not acquire land. Finally, in 1878, at the Congress of Berlin, the Great Powers of Europe made Romania's independence conditional upon the granting of civil rights to the Jews. But Jews were still subject to oppressive naturalization procedures, and anti-Semitism continued unabated.

The Jewish community, which was largely urban and consisted primarily of those of Russian and Polish descent, became increasingly organized at the end of the nineteenth century. The first Jewish representative body in Romania, the Brotherhood of Zion society, was founded in 1872 under the influence of Benjamin Franklin Peixotto, the first American diplomat in Romania. A Jewish school system was founded in 1893, after Jews were expelled from the public schools. And the noted Russian Jewish playwright Abraham Goldfaden started the world's first professional Yiddish theater company in Romania in 1876.

Anti-Semitism grew throughout the 1920s and 1930s. After Hitler came to power in Germany in 1933, Romania's fascist Iron Guard also adopted anti-Semitic policies. Romania entered World War II on the side of the Germans in 1941, and it is estimated that between 280,000 and 380,000 Jews were killed. Even though the majority of Romanian Jews survived the war, a commission established by former Romanian president Ion Iliescu determined that Romania was responsible for the deaths of more Jews than any country other than Germany itself.

After the war, many Romanian Jews immigrated to Palestine, including the Nobel Prize–winning author Elie Wiesel and the noted Israeli writer Aharon Appelfeld. There are between 9,000 and 15,000 Jews living in Romania today.

Russian

Russian-Jewish army officers at a Passover seder in 1905,
during the Russo-Japanese War.

(William Sriro / YIVO Institute for Jewish Research, New York)

Chem otlichayetsya eta noch´ ot vsekh drugikh nochei?

Vo vse drugiye nochi my yedim kvasnoi khleb i matsu;
v etu noch´, tol´ko matsu.

Vo vse drugiye nochi my yedim lyubuyu zelen´;
v etu noch´, tol´ko gor´kuyu.

Vo vse drugiye nochi my ni razu ne obmakivayem;
v etu noch´, obmakivayem dvazhdy.

Vo vse drugiye nochi my yedim sidya ili vozlezha;
v etu noch´, vse vozlezhim.

Чем отличается эта ночь от всех других ночей?

Во все другие ночи мы едим квасной хлеб и мацу;
в эту ночь, только мацу.

Во все другие ночи мы едим любую зелень;
в эту ночь, только горькую.

Во все другие ночи мы ни разу не обмакиваем;
в эту ночь, обмакиваем дважды.

Во все другие ночи мы едим сидя или возлежа;
в эту ночь, все возлежим.

THE JEWS OF RUSSIA

THE EARLIEST RECORD of a Jewish presence in Russia dates back to the fourth century. The Khazars, a Turkic people from Central Asia who ruled much of the region, adopted Judaism in the eighth century. After the overthrow of the Khazars by ethnic Russians in 969, Jews fled the Crimea in large numbers. In the eleventh and twelfth centuries they settled in Kiev. The Jewish population increased in the fourteenth century, when many Jews came to Eastern Europe fleeing persecution in England, France, and Spain.

In the sixteenth century, Tsar Ivan IV ("Ivan the Terrible") subjected the Jews to persecution and expulsion, and for centuries thereafter the policies of tsarist Russia were openly anti-Semitic. In the late eighteenth century, Catherine the Great began to establish restrictions on where Jews could live and work, and in 1835, Tsar Nicholas I limited the area where Jews were permitted to live to a region known as the Pale of Settlement. There Jews were confined to small towns and villages called shtetls. Throughout the nineteenth century, the Jews of Russia were persecuted in government-sponsored riots known as pogroms. The pogroms escalated in 1881, when Jews were falsely blamed for the assassination of Tsar Alexander II.

More than two million Jews fled Russia between 1880 and 1920. Most emigrated to the United States, although several thousand went to Palestine. Jews continued to flee Russia when the pogroms escalated in 1903, and then again during the Russian Revolution of 1917, when the Bolsheviks seized power under Lenin.

Although both Lenin and Stalin officially spoke out against anti-Semitism, the Soviet Union was hostile toward Jewish religious and cultural institutions. More than one million Soviet Jews were murdered during the Holocaust, both in mass shootings and in death camps. Another 200,000 Jews were killed while fighting in the Red Army against the Nazis. Following the war, discrimination against Jews continued; it is believed that only the death of Stalin in 1953 prevented a full-scale massacre of Soviet Jews. Although the Soviet Union recognized the establishment of the State of Israel in 1948, the government refused to grant emigration visas to Soviet Jews who wanted to move to Israel and subjected them to discrimination and imprisonment.

Despite the centuries of persecution, Russian Jews had an astonishingly rich religious and cultural life. Noted Jews living in tsarist Russia and the Soviet Union include Rabbi Eliyahu ben Shlomo Zalman, the legendary Lithuanian Talmudic sage who was known as the Vilna Gaon; Sholom Rabinovich, the chronicler of shtetl life who was known as Sholem Aleichem; the Yiddish poet Kadia Molodowsky; and the actor and director Solomon Mikhoels, who was murdered by Stalin's agents in 1948.

With the collapse of the U.S.S.R. in 1991, more than one million Soviet Jews left for Israel, Germany, and America. Because many choose to keep their religious identity secret, it is hard to say how many Jews live in Russia today, but the number is believed to be between 300,000 and 500,000.

Spanish

Each family member is performing a different seder ritual in this illustration from what has come to be known as the Sarajevo Haggadah. This handwritten and beautifully illustrated Haggadah actually originated in Barcelona in the middle of the fourteenth century, which makes it the oldest Sephardic Haggadah in existence. It was bought by the National Museum in Sarajevo in 1894, where it is now on permanent display. In 1991, it was appraised at seven hundred million dollars.

(Beth Hatefutsoth Photo Archive, Tel Aviv)

¿Porque es esta noche diferente a
cualquier otra noche?

En otras noches comemos pan leudado y pan ácimo;
esa noche se come solo el pan ácimo.

En otras noches comemos cualquier tipo de vegetal;
esa noche se comen solo las hierbas agrias.

En otras noches no mojamos nuestra comida ni una sola vez;
esa noche se moja la comida dos veces.

En otras noches se come sentados rectamente ó reclinado;
esa noche cenamos sentados todos reclinados.

THE JEWS OF SPAIN

THE EARLIEST JEWISH presence in Spain dates back to the third century C.E., when Jews were accepted as full citizens of the Roman Empire. By the fifth century, the region was overrun by barbarian invaders from Western Europe and came under the rule of the Germanic Visigoths, who, when they converted to Christianity, gave the Jews the option of conversion or expulsion

Muslims from North Africa invaded the Iberian Peninsula in 711 C.E., and throughout the period of Moorish rule (from the eighth through the twelfth centuries), the Jews of Spain openly practiced their religion and thrived both culturally and economically. The reign of Abd-al-Rahman III in the tenth century marked the start of the golden age of Spanish Jewry. Jews made notable contributions in the fields of philosophy, logic, mathematics, medicine, and astronomy. Famous Sephardic scholars of this period include the Jewish councillor and court physician Hasdai ibn Shaprut; the poets Yehuda ha-Levi and Solomon ibn Gavirol; the Bible commentator and scientist Moses ibn Ezra; and the doctor, philosopher, and Bible commentator Moses ben Maimon (Maimonides), a towering figure of medieval Torah scholarship.

The fate of the Jews deteriorated during the Reconquista, the Christian reconquest of Spain. In 1267, an order from Pope Clement IV resulted in the persecution of converted Jews suspected of practicing their religion in secret, and of those Jews who were thought to exercise undue influence over Christians and new converts. Anti-Semitism increased into the fourteenth century, with major massacres taking place in 1366 and 1391. Thousands of Jews were forced to convert to Christianity and became known as *conversos* or Marranos (Spanish for "swine"). Throughout Castile, Jews were forced to inhabit separate quarters and grow their hair and beards so that they would look different from the Christian population. This period of great persecution was known as the Inquisition, and culminated in the expulsion of the Jews from Spain in the summer of 1492. It is estimated that between 100,000 and 250,000 Jews were expelled.

From 1492 to 1868, the only Jews living in Spain were Marranos. Many retained their Jewish identities in secret while professing to be Catholic in public. In 1869, the Spanish government created a new constitution granting religious tolerance. Jews began to return to Spain, and synagogues were opened in Madrid and Barcelona. But the official edict of expulsion was not repealed until 1968.

From 1933 until the outbreak of the Spanish Civil War in 1936, about 3,000 Jewish refugees from Nazi Germany fled to Spain. During World War II, the government of Francisco Franco allowed more than 25,000 Jews to use the country as an escape route from the war in Europe. After the war, improved economic and social conditions attracted an increasing number of Jews to Spain. There are about 30,000 Jews in Spain today, mostly Sephardim who emigrated from North Africa.

Swedish

Holocaust survivors who have been brought to Sweden, at their first
Passover seder after being liberated from concentration camps, 1946.

*(Beth Hatefutsoth Photo Archive, Tel Aviv.
Courtesty of Judiska Kvinnoklubben, Stockholm)*

Varför är denna natt olik alla andra nätter?

På alla andra nätter äta vi syrat och osyrat;
denna natt endast osyrat.

På alla andra nätter äta vi allehanda slags örter;
denna natt bittra örter.

På alla andra nätter doppa vi icke ens en gång;
denna natt två gånger.

På alla andra nätter äta vi såväl sittande som lutade;
denna natt vi alla lutade.

THE FIRST OFFICIAL Jewish community in Sweden was established in the 1770s when Aaron Isaac, an engraver from Germany, was granted permission to settle in the country with his family. Prior to that, Jews had to convert to Christianity before they were permitted to settle there. Swedish Jews were subjected to immigration restrictions and to restrictions on what kind of work they could do. They were forbidden to intermarry and, until 1860, Jews were permitted to live in only a few designated cities. But from the very beginning, Swedish Jews were given basic religious freedom and the right to administer their own affairs.

In 1838, the Jews were incorporated into the Swedish state as "adherents of the Mosaic faith." This decree led to their acceptance as free citizens who were no longer restricted to particular occupations. They were allowed to acquire real estate and to participate in municipal elections. In the latter half of the nineteenth century, Jews played a major role in the cultural life of the nation, especially in the fields of music, painting, and literary criticism. Not surprisingly, many Swedish Jews began to assimilate. They modeled their synagogue services after those of German Reform Jewry. The prayer service was shortened, and sermons were delivered in Swedish rather than Hebrew. Around the turn of the twentieth century, many Jews immigrated to

Sweden from Eastern Europe, bringing the Jewish population to 7,000 by 1930.

Sweden was considered neutral during World War II, and the Swedish people became involved in many efforts to save European Jews during the Holocaust. In 1942, Sweden allowed 900 Norwegian Jews to immigrate. The following year, the country granted asylum to the entire Danish Jewish community of 8,000, who arrived in Sweden during the night, in small fishing boats. The Swedish diplomat Raoul Wallenberg saved thousands of Hungarian Jews in Budapest. The Nobel Prize–winning poet Nelly Sachs, born in Berlin, arrived in Sweden as a refugee in 1940 and spent the rest of her life in Stockholm.

The Jewish population of Sweden doubled between 1945 and 1970, as the country continued to accept thousands of refugees. In 1951, a new law granting freedom of religion to all citizens enabled Jews to hold public office for the first time. More recently, Sweden has become a pioneer in Holocaust education: In November 1997, the Swedish government introduced a large-scale educational program called the Living History Project, which involved distributing a free book about the Holocaust to every household in the nation. Sweden has also been very supportive of Israel, and the two countries have strong economic and cultural ties. There are about 18,000 Jews living in Sweden today.

Turkish

This drawing of a Jewish cloth merchant from Turkey was originally published, in 1568, in *Les Quatre Premiers Livres des Navigations et Peregrinations Orientales* (The First Four Books of Navigations and Peregrinations in the Orient), a travel book by the cartographer Nicolas de Nicolay.

(Beth Hatefutsoth Photo Archive, Tel Aviv)

Bu gece diğer gecelerden ne kadar değişiktir?

Diğer geceler bir kere bile banmayız;
bu gece ise iki kere banarız.

Diğer geceler mayalı ve mayasız ekmek yeriz;
bu gece ise yalnız mayasız ekmek yeriz.

Diğer geceler çeşitli yeşillikler yeriz;
bu gece ise yalnız marul yeriz.

Diğer geceler oturarak ya da yaslanarak yemek yeriz;
bu gece ise hepimiz ziyafetteki davetliler gibi
yaslanarak yemek yeriz.

THE JEWS OF TURKEY

JEWISH LIFE in Asia Minor dates back to the fourth century B.C.E. The Christian rulers of the Byzantine Empire persecuted the Jews living there for centuries, but the situation improved when the Ottoman Turks conquered the area. The first Jewish community to come under Ottoman rule was Bursa, which was captured in 1326. Jews in Bursa were permitted to build synagogues, conduct business, and purchase houses. In 1453, the Ottoman sultan captured Constantinople, which became the capital of the empire. From then on, whenever the sultan captured a town, its Jews were transferred to Constantinople, where a wealthy Jewish community began to flourish.

Over the centuries, an increasing number of European Jews fleeing persecution in their native lands found refuge in Turkey. Four Turkish cities—Istanbul (formerly Constantinople), Izmir, Safed, and Salonica—became centers of Sephardic Jewry. In 1493, Istanbul became home to one of the first Hebrew printing presses. Jewish literature flourished throughout the empire: Rabbi Joseph Caro compiled the *Shulchan Aruch*, the definitive code of Jewish law; and Shlomo HaLevi Alkabes composed "Lekhah Dodi," a song welcoming the Sabbath.

The situation of the Jews throughout the Ottoman Empire deteriorated in the seventeenth century under the rule of the intolerant Sultan Murad III. Jews were forced to wear special clothing and to live in segregated areas. During this difficult period, a Jewish Turk named Shabbtai Zevi claimed to be the Messiah. Zevi attracted a large group of followers throughout Europe. But he eventually converted to Islam, as did many of his followers.

The eighteenth century was a period of general cultural decline among the Jews of Turkey, most of whom could no longer understand Hebrew. Turkish Jews began writing and publishing in Ladino instead.

In 1856, a decree aimed at reforming the Ottoman Empire declared that all its citizens, including the Jews, were equal under the law. But with the start of World War I, the Ottoman Empire declined even further. It was replaced by the Turkish Republic and then, in 1923, by modern-day Turkey. The Turkish language was introduced in the schools, and Jews began speaking and writing in Turkish for the first time.

During World War II, Turkey maintained neutrality and became a safe haven for Jews fleeing Nazi persecution. Following the war, many Turkish Jews immigrated to Palestine. Today, most of the Jews in Turkey live in Istanbul. They are legally represented by a chief rabbi known as the Haham Bashi, a position that has existed for centuries. There are about 26,000 Jews in Turkey today, most of them Sephardic.

Yiddish

This photograph was taken at the inauguration of the first
Yiddish school in Dvinsk, Latvia, in 1914. The guest of honor
in the center is the writer Sholem Aleichem.

(I. Levin-Shatzkes / YIVO Institute for Jewish Research, New York)

Farvos iz de nakht fun Pesakh andersh fun aleh nekht fun a gantz yohr?

Aleh nekht fun a gantz yohr esen mir khometz un matzah;
ober di nakht fun Pesakh esen mir nor matzah.

Aleh nekht fun a gantz yohr esen mir alerlay grinsen;
ober di nakht fun Pesakh esen mir nor bitereh grinsen.

Aleh nekht fun a gantz yohr tunken mir nit on afiloo ayn mohl;
ober di nakht fun Pesakh tunken mir tzvey mohl.

Aleh nekht fun a gantz yohr esen mir sai zitzenkik un sai ongelent;
ober di nakht fun Pesakh esen mir nor ongelent.

פאַרוואָס איז די נאַכט פֿון פּסח אַנדערש פֿון אַלע
נעכט פֿון אַ גאַנץ יאָר?

אַלע נעכט פֿון אַ גאַנץ יאָר עסן מיר חמץ און מצה;
אָבער די נאַכט פֿון פּסח עסן מיר נאָר מצה.

אַלע נעכט פֿון אַ גאַנץ יאָר עסן מיר אַלערלײַ גרינסן;
אָבער די נאַכט פֿון פּסח עסן מיר נאָר ביטערע גרינסן.

אַלע נעכט פֿון אַ גאַנץ יאָר טונקן מיר ניט אָן אַפֿילו אײן מאָל;
אָבער די נאַכט פֿון פּסח טונקן מיר צוויי מאָל.

אַלע נעכט פֿון אַ גאַנץ יאָר עסן מיר סיי זיצנדיק און סיי אָנגעלענט;
אָבער די נאַכט פֿון פּסח עסן מיר נאָר אָנגעלענט.

YIDDISH

YIDDISH, a Germanic language written in Hebrew characters, has been spoken by European Jews for more than a thousand years.

Yiddish arose between the ninth and twelfth centuries in south-western Germany. It began as a dialect of what is now known as Middle High German, to which were added Hebrew words pertaining to Jewish religious life. Later, when European Jews moved eastward, the Yiddish language acquired Slavic-language influences as well.

Early Yiddish literature consisted mostly of religious works intended to make Judaism accessible to common people. These include, most famously, the *Tz'enah Ur'enah*, an anthology of passages from the Bible, Talmud, and Midrash intended for women, which was composed by Jacob ben Isaac Askenazi in early-seventeenth-century Poland. For a brief period in the late fifteenth and sixteenth centuries, Ashkenazic Jews living in Northern Italy created a rich secular literature of epic poetry and satire. But this literature gradually disappeared as the Jews assimilated into Italian society and culture.

While Hebrew always remained the language of Jewish prayer, the rise of Hasidism in the eighteenth century led to the more widespread use of Yiddish in an attempt to spread Jewish learning among the less educated. The stories of the great Hasidic master the Ba'al Shem Tov, for instance, were written in Yiddish. The Haskalah (Jewish Enlightenment) also led to a more widespread use of Yiddish in an attempt to familiarize Jews with secular Western culture, even though the leaders of the Haskalah looked down upon Yiddish as a corrupt German dialect.

A rich secular Yiddish literature developed in Eastern Europe in the late nineteenth and early twentieth centuries. The three most famous writers of this period were Sholom Jacob Abramowitz (known as Mendele Mokher Seforim), Sholom Rabinovich (known as Sholem Aleichem), and Isaac Leib Peretz. These authors wrote stories about life in the shtetl.

At the start of the twentieth century, Yiddish was emerging as a major Eastern European language: A rich Yiddish literature was being published; Yiddish theater and film were extremely popular; and formal Yiddish-language education became more widespread. After 1914, however, traditional Jewish life in Eastern Europe began to decline under the impact of wars, migrations, revolutions, and persecutions. Many Yiddish writers fled to the United States and settled in New York City, among them the Nobel Prize–winning author I. B. Singer.

On the eve of World War II, there were eleven million Yiddish speakers worldwide. But the destruction of Eastern European Jewish communities during the Holocaust led to a dramatic, sudden decline in the use of Yiddish, a process that continued with increased assimilation and the rise of modern Hebrew. The YIVO Institute for Jewish Research, founded in Vilna in 1925 and reestablished in New York in 1940, is a repository of archival material for the preservation of the language, literature, and culture of the Jews of Eastern Europe. The National Yiddish Book Center, located in Amherst, Massachusetts, has rescued more than one million Yiddish books that were about to be discarded and has made collections of Yiddish literature available to university libraries throughout the United States.

Today, Yiddish is spoken by about half a million people around the world, most of whom are Orthodox Jews.

Acknowledgments

MUCH OF the historical information in this book is taken from the *Encyclopedia Judaica*. The following Web sites also provided valuable historical background: www.haruth .com/JewsoftheWorld.html and www.jewishvirtuallibrary.org/jsource.

I would like to thank the following individuals for their scholarly advice and generous assistance: Dr. Stephen Donshik, Aryeh Doobov, Philip Elman, Michael Glatzer of the Yad Ben Zvi Institute, Dr. Miriam Goldstein, Dr. Alisa Rubin Kurshan, Ariella Kurshan, Jenny Labendz, Zippi Rosenne of Beth Hatefutsoth, Dr. Shuly Rubin Schwartz, Iddo Winter, and Dr. Tzemah Yoreh. For providing the translations and transliterations, my thanks to Misha Beletsky, Tracy Cabanis, Efterpe Dakoglou, Noreen Daniel, Romiel Daniel, Professor Jeremy Dauber, Anne Díaz, Karen Emmerich, Jasmin Farhangian, Jasper Frank, Professor Chris Harwood, Rachel Tessler Karper, Victoria Lu, Dr. Negist Mengesha, Isaac Meyers, Professor Mona Momescu, Haim Rimenberg, Crismeylin Rivano, Johanna Roebas, Jennifer Snodgrass, Anke Steinecke, Chayah Tessler, Professor Daniel Tsadik, Bozena Wawrzonek, and Alex Zlotnick. Some of the transliterations come from *A*

Different Night: The Leader's Guide to The Family Participation Haggadah, by Noam Zion and David Dishon (Jerusalem: Shalom Hartman Institute, 1997), pages 25–27. Special thanks to Beth Hatefutsoth, The Nahum Goldmann Museum of the Jewish Diaspora, Tel Aviv.

Deepest thanks to my infinitely dedicated editor and mentor, Altie Karper, who made this book happen.